BALANCING ACTS

BALANCING ACTS

POEMS BY

ROBIN SEYFRIED

EASTERN WASHINGTON UNIVERSITY PRESS

SPOKANE, WASHINGTON 2000

Author photo by Mike Urban
Cover photo from the Harry Hertzberg Circus Collection,
    San Antonio Public Library
Cover and book design by Scott Poole

Library of Congress Cataloging-in-Publication Data
Seyfried, Robin—
Balancing Acts / by Robin Seyfried
p. cm.
ISBN 0-910055-64-5 (pbk.)
I. Title
PS3569.E8866 B3 2000
811'.54--dc21   99-059812

These poems are for my family—

for my mother and father,

for David, Ali, and Addy—

with love and thanks.

FROM THE HOME OFFICE

THE WIVES OF THE POETS

This bard was mad and this one
and so were they all for that matter
this one drank this one hated
his father and so did they all
ask their wives their good
wives their house

                    wives
and this one taught this one
cried this one was lost
one went all the way
home   again and again
this one knew the way
this one's mother left
and so did they

                 didn't they
just love their love
poems didn't they all give their all
for that matter

               don't ask
their wives their mothers their temperate daughters
their cold sullen sons

                  this one wanted
a muse a mistress a woman to mis-
treat an apple a fish an old wife
a midwife will tell you *my own was the best*
or the worst

             depending

and the wives of the poets
loved them regardless   in spite
of their faults their needs
their abuses their incessant tuneless singing

and this one died and so

did they all   dead drunk   for that mattter
dead broke   dead still and all over
America   all over the Western World the wives
of the poets
                    in hardcover and paper
on nightstands in kitchens in classrooms
on couches and coffeetables
the wives of the poets are having the last

words.

BULK POETRY

Someone's very pretty
daughter at the block party
tells me she wants to be
a writer
                    so I ask politely
which genre   immediately
apologizing   you're young you don't need
to limit yourself but she's already
written *a thousand poems*
and six short stories and maybe
tossing her tawny hair
a novel but I need more life
experience first—maybe
you just need
                    gall I say
which reminds me
even poor Emily
only managed about one a day
all that long dark year she thought
she was a goner—though my own cousin
told me he'd written over
a hundred poems in two weeks
last summer and on TV
New Year's Eve two local
personalities are giving their
numbers up for posterity:
four hundred for the one named Cindy
and *praise God*   she's only
going to read the one   meanwhile
it's 1997 and I have no idea how many
I've written   I'd better
get busy.

After the specific birds
and places, the moon songs, shards
and other ruins,
after the endings, the weather,
deaths little and large,
come the numbered questions:
>   *Why that particular bird?*
>   *Why this word? Why not*
>   *rhyme? What would happen*
>   *if the hawk were a robin? or an eagle?*
>   *Can you imagine . . . ?*
A textbook case, open and shut,
of the poem—or more often
the poet—as problem:
>   *Why was this written?*

Remember the schoolboy, the doctor's son,
who called you and your husband
at ten-thirty one evening—unaware
you were lying down—to demand
>   *Where is personification?*
>   *What is imagery?*
>   and whether your poems ever
>   meant more than they were saying.
>   *Was this* just *about flying?*
>   *Could an* image *be a person?*
What's wrong with this picture?
All in the name of *metonymy synecdoche*
anapest and *simile* from *alba* to *zeugma*
amen.   The search and destroy
method of teaching.   Remember
his project was due the next morning.
He needed the answers.

WHERE DO YOU GET YOUR IDEAS?

—perennial question at poetry readings

I often find them left
    on the answering
machine garbled and half-
    erased or just before
(your name here) the beep
    a friend in another
state sounding vaguely
    familiar or behind
warped doors in the in
    and out boxes under
the desk clipped to accounts
    payable torn from nap-
kins misplaced with the match
    books tucked behind my ear
mixed with pocket fuzz at the bottom
    of an old purse in mothballs
in the pantry with pasta
    and carpet beetles forgotten
at the back of the freezer
                        Some
times they show up suddenly
    like dust-studded cobwebs and
shirttail relations between a rock
    and a hard place in the concrete
drive or in unnamed files on the hard
    drive stuck to my right shoe
under restaurant tables in actuarial
    tables obituaries inside
the inside out unmatched black
    sock in the laundry basket or sprouting
on the white grout brushing
    my husband's bare forearm

the dog's soft silver belly
    in the lint trap
               and some nights
when I look in
    on my sleeping children
I find them
    warm and damp warbling
beneath the covers.

PORTRAIT OF THE ARTIST

for Dan

Drawn fine
hard
    as wire
he wants
        nothing
food no words no
water his hands

used to line-drawing
the still lives
of ink and paper
fall now from
tender wrists
       so
smooth so new
they keep time
at arm's length

his night-fed
        eyes
already have turned
away
    fierce beauty
down to bone

he won't be
touched   wants to
get it over with
out breaking
his concentration
without losing
control   the only

thing now   touching
          being
touched
          be done

done with this dying

this lost art

LESSONS IN ART CRITICISM

for Addy

Not quite five   she thinks
                         it's a dog
the frazzled blowsy
Ward Corley bouquet
in the master
                    bedroom
has called it *that dog*
since she was three

See: FLOWERS   I say
the spectral corollas dried
     falling   becoming
shades of meaning
          gossamer and dusk
                                    just
getting good the artist said

               Then why she says
did he paint a nose
and eyes and white
hair?
          The storm blue hearts
of ghost blossoms now stare
               at me too
the damp nose quivers
you're right   I say

your dog ate
my flowers

FOR ADDY, THREE AND A HALF YEARS

Suddenly she turns
                    to me
looking up
            my younger
daughter, saying *When I bees*
five I'm gonna ride
the bus with Alex
                        I nod and keep
driving   *bees* I think re-
membering that persistent hum
the hive tight and sweet
around the heart knot yielding
the power *there* down my arm
in my palm: names verbs wordzzzzz—

But Mommy?
                I return
There's no buckles
on the bus so Alex
is gonna save me. She nods
She gonna put her arms around me so I be
safe
      Are you sad

Mommy? I shake my head
at the road   That's good
I say   I want this faith
to last as long
as possible: this world
without buckles
where you can be safe
in someone's arms.

NATURE LESSON

for Alexandra

My daughter has gone next door
with her father and spiders (take two
round crackers, peanut butter, raisins
for eyes and eight pretzel-stick
legs): an offering to Katy the golden
third-grader, in hopes she'll be asked in
to play.   My daughter has gone

next door and returned years older.
She stands now beside me, her narrow
shoulders—struck suddenly with the weight
of six years—shudder. *What's wrong?*
I put my arm around her as she sobs
in gusts.   We are helpless—she and I
and her father—to explain why the plate
dropped and the spiders jumped

all over with kind Theresa overlooking
the carnage of sticks and crumbs
in her spotless entryway, turning a blind
eye to the raisins and saying how
nice would you like to come in? And *no
thank you* said my daughter more politely
and sadly than ever before.

My fault, I think. What natural mother
sends spiders to a neighbor—
even in October, even wrapped in pink
plastic on flowered paper? We sway slightly
while she cries.   I say to myself Why
didn't you go in? *I forgot
what I wanted* is her answer.

So we stand, my firstbo:n daughter—
not flesh of my flesh yet heart
of my heart—taking this beating
together.

THREE WISHES

for Ali

Bird Millman was the first American wire artiste to perform without the aid of a balancing umbrella. A favorite of the 1920s, the dainty and vivacious performer sang solos as she danced the wire.
              —Photo caption from *Pictorial History of the American Circus* by John and Alice Durant

I.

At dinner you ask me what
is a godmother   my almost ten
year old daughter (you've been
almost ten for about
a year now)
              before I can answer
a fairy godmother?   you tease
                              relying
like me   on the old stories
the old banter
in your case a Sherry godmother
we laugh
         how to explain
I believe in the office, the person
if not the tradition
    I try again   No
a fairy grants three wishes
and is done   a godmother
grants wishes   bears gifts
forever
         and once upon ago
I saw my best friend
uneasy at your dedication

you, wriggling in a long white gown
water from a yellow rose
on your brow
your monumental scowl
(you are always
the princess every Halloween no matter
how many other career choices I offer)
then as now
you made me wonder

II.

Because you are so much more
my love my lovely seer
than your present struggle
with the times tables six through nine
or your latest spelling score
because you cry you want
to impress me
I go looking for a fairy
to tell your future
and find instead an old photo:
black and white
light and shadow
a woman: Bird
Millman on tiptoe
on a wire   caught
mid-crossing
ribboned slippers and soft wings
of hair everything else
the background a blur
but her face in profile
calmly looking down

her weight informs the wire
an arc, a bow, a sine
that travels with her constant

and a flash
of recognition: her poise
and passion   her straight
and narrow path   demanding
precision   her chosen
work which is hard
and absurd and worth
every moment

III.

You have more gifts
than you yet know: one deep
dimple and cleft chin
from your birthmother
long skillful hands from your birthfather
and your own blue
eyes   blue of dusk and spark
of summer storms
which have always seen
                              inside
your artless artful nature
your dark and bright
                        what more
could any kind of mother make
but wishes:
              you will know
the meaning of tensile strength:
      that a woman may stretch
and stretch without breaking
without being torn

let your left shoulder
never rise to cover fear
but at the end
of every question may you find
your own unfettered heart

whole and certain
                    above all
you will find uncommon grace
like that woman who
with no umbrella
for balance or shelter
and dressed in thin chiffon
trimmed with feathers
still sang solos
as she danced
the wire

SONGS OF INEXPERIENCE

DANCING ATTENDANCE

Let's see you
dance, she says.
You're not dancing
she says as I try
to shuffle off. She's calling
the shots.

I begin to toe
the line, slowly heel
over. I put my right
foot in, my best foot
forward and suddenly my feet
don't matter   I am dancing on
air, all night, in the dark, cheek
to cheek   hoofing it for all
I'm worth   Pavlova
through Isadora having a highland
fling   no accompaniment but
the limbs, in time:
glissade, *jeté*, and bump,
                        grind,
                        and one
for Giselle and two
for the swan—
I'm dying again
to please the audience.

                    But just
when I think I've given
my all, I'm ready to take it
home, to go for the roses, the big
finish, she says:

Now sing. She says,
let's hear you
sing.

THE PROOF

She claimed it was water
but I knew by her fingers
the *pit pit*   the smell
as she screwed the pincurls
into my skull
my mother put spit
on my hair
creating order
producing a chorus of commas
on my forehead that meant

pause   wait   walk   don't

stomp swing gallop slide
for home kiss Steve kick John
for tearing my sash rip his pocket
crash against the backstop hit
the dirt play horses mustangs
forever the fastest on the playground—

and sooner or later the hairdo
came undone.
It's all there in kindergarten,
the class picture: my eyes down,
hair blunt, bangs a geyser,
my father's thin smile.
I knew I'd catch hell.

Patty's mother did it to her
too. You could tell
the way hers waved

stiffly, all the same frequency.
There was something wrong
with her legs that didn't show
beneath the frilly hemline
above the perfectly white
anklets and glassy MaryJanes.
She wasn't supposed to run.
She was fragile.
In the picture you can see
every hair in place, each unnatural
curl. But then Patty

was a good girl.

GENESIS, FIFTH GRADE

As you were Jehovah's Witness, you had me pegged
for a sinner even then, before my first
decade was up. Whatever my original sin—maybe
our mutual crush on Mr. Elmquist—I recall
your wrath. Even now when I open my revised standard
version Oxford Annotated you appear to me,
all blonde ponytail, curly bangs, gingham
and fists, crying "I bet you don't even know the name
of the first book in the Bible," exposing me
for a Congregationalist in name only,
my quiz-kid confidence stuck
to my undershirt.

Annetta, it is countless grades
later. Neither of us is a virgin.
You are married, have already given
birth, and I am still trying
to answer you: I have learned
long since that the Good Book
is a good book, that writers may be divinely
inspired but editors often
aren't, that one man's shepherds
are another's wise men and translation
is its own reward (witness King James'
unicorn), that walking on water is old
hat to Buddha and just ask his mother
about immaculate conceptions. Above all,
I've learned that metaphor works
in mysterious ways and I'm still a long,
long way from Revelation.

THE NATIONAL ANTHEM

I could hit the high notes, I said,
the ones at the top of the Star-
Spangled Banner and the teacher said yes, yes,
you may lead today and I jumped for the first bar
and it was fine, a little high maybe, but wasn't it
fine when I sang *OH-o say* with the whole class
behind me, Mrs. Kipp's sixth graders: Richard who just
that day said I was flat, and Donelyn with breasts the object
of all our desires. I could see they were all
for me: Junelle, Annetta, and Betty
who'd never seen snow, Warren, and Kim the musical
genius, soft Shawn, and Karen the new girl, and Debbie
who told Karen to avoid me—in it together
at the twilight's last—buck-toothed Frank and Bernard the reverse
swallower always gargling 'round the rugged rocks, fragile
Patty whose grandpa was buried with our get well
cards—my brave classmates, still with me at *the ramparts*
and after *so gallantly streaming* it was no good
going back, too late to stop, nowhere to go
but up, up to the inevitable *rockets'*
red glare and up once more with *the bombs*
bursting and down Oh god back down *through the night*, grateful
that our flag was still there, bracing myself for the final
ascent toward *the land of the free*—a height
my thin soprano barely reached and where I knew no one
would follow.

I still sing it softly at ball games,
changing keys with the crowd or taking cover
under some great Voice. But they come back:
thirty faces straining for the one *glare,* even Mrs. Kipp's

chevron smile flagging as she heard where I intended
to take them. Thirty red faces for my solo breaking
free, for the shame of starting too high
and finishing alone.

HANGING ON

for Mother

I.

There are leaves in the poems now,
a crisp yielding underfoot.
It is killing time
that matters to the Muse:
the mumbling withered bitch,
snoose chinked in her teeth,
demands a kiss,
a kiss for her ripe old age.

Here is the endless fall
dreams hold.
The last leaves are tanned,
scattered like cereal on the ground.
Death: breakfast of champions.
Here is morning
shaken from a rumpled sky.

It is the season for deadlines,
for the nagging scent of mulch, leaves
pulled or blasted into glittering heaps.
Now dormancy
grazes the spine, branches
drowse and scrape against walls
as the Muse plays trick or treat,
her knock promising no one
at the door.

II.

Your Chicken Soup Ethic/
my Puritan Work.
You clump into my poems
iambic with gout,
bringing ice cream, scotch,
ripe colors on pavement—
a cornucopia of comfort.

Tell me you love autumn
and do not appreciate death:
In all this wind
there must be something
that falls, that clings
breathless.

III.

But the leaves—
you must understand the leaves
are turning:
spun to claws in the cutting air,
splayed on wet walks
making steps uncertain,
turning for another fall.

Turn,
fall,
slapstick choreography
for a broken-nosed ballerina.
Here is the dance that holds the mind
still, the holding out
of imagery for its afterbirth,
for the fullness of decay.

BEDTIME STORIES

for my father

I remember nights full of leaves and your voice
guiding me through *The Jungle Books*, your long frame
pinched in my small rocking chair. Those nights
there were no bones under the bed; you and Mother
weren't dead in the next room.

Of all the creatures you named into being, only two
remain. Last night, I had to look up Kaa the wise
python, big effusive Baloo the bear, and corrupt
Shere Khan the tiger. Only the child, Mowgli, and Bagheera
came without my calling.

Bagheera—the low, purring syllables still conjure
the panther, the prickly shadow of fear. It was Bagheera
I knew best: he made Mowgli laugh, his playfulness
brought pain, his silence was a warning.
Sleek, strong Bagheera sheathed both anger

and joy. Sarcastic Bagheera mocked the elephant's
boasting, the tale that "had not lost fat
in the telling." His lessons were lean, his whisper
meant danger. His praise was like water in the dry
season. Proud, lonely Bagheera could never

meet Mowgli's eyes. When the cub was grown,
it was Bagheera who ran from the parting, calling
"Remember, Bagheera loved thee. Remember Bagheera
loved thee." Night after night, it was Bagheera
who carried me safely into sleep on his hard, dark back.

ALWAYS THE CAMELS

Motherless Sundays and Daddy's good girl
at the parks and museums   the grey art museum
its hard floors flat paintings
the long empty rooms   *just look*
at small lessons in jade   *never touch*
the stone faces   the masks   looking always
for words   learning wall after wall

but outside were camels
                        two Ming marble camels
for climbing for stroking for waiting your turn
to be lifted up giddy
to undulant stillness   that place in the middle worn new
with the years with the pressing desires
of stiff-legged riders   thighs grasping fullness
and rough welcome chill
                        of the dynastic camels
keeping their distance   grave guarding camels
taken from tombs
                 the decorous dispossessed dumb beasts
of burden   belonging to no one   set fast
and set free

There were other excursions when mother worked weekends
the dams and fishladders   a petrified forest
all special exhibits   all one of a kind   only one
in a lifetime   the firstborn the last   like the mother
like father like daughter like son
                     and what wasn't easy
for Daddy's big daddy's bright daddy's best
girl
        always the camels   the reaching toward silence
the distance   the cold space   the long
hard ride.

THE SEMAPHORE OF FATHERS

Some fathers are open around the clock,
some crouch like catchers at 4 and 8,
some start with arms at 9 and 3, then reach
straight out to pull you in.
Some give their blessing at 2 and 10.
Some are rigidly 6 for wait-and-see.
Some cheer you on at 11 and 1.

One waits alone at the end of a ramp
at the end of a journey,
his hands held ready at 5 and 7,
palms turned out, meaning *I have been hurt*
but it wasn't you   I know that
now   I had nothing
to hide.   If you ask he will open
to 3 and 9, meaning *all along—*

that one is mine.

SONG FOR WHAT FELL TO THE FLOOR

The first woman wouldn't do it   couldn't
make the first cut singing OH No
you'll cry but the next one bunched it   chopped
it just below the neck in her fist   see
I'm not crying   but there was that sick
squeak and crunch when the scissors
met again and two voices behind
me singing Oh NO it was so long so
thick   two grey ladies shouting dryer
to dryer with me sitting there like some fresh
amputee   they're singing no   I can still feel it
brush along my spine   I can't see
that it's gone and yes well there
you have it: so hot over the collar so heavy   in
the movies they pull just one pin and it's
down and they're off but I'd be
pulling pins all night.

Now there it is all behind me
beneath me   it's just an old plaything
a skein he used to like to unwind   an excuse
for gestures   tics really   it's not there now
when my hand flips it behind my shoulder   there
now   just a warm place where I changed
expressions   always in the way   but it's so long
to the tangles   goodbye to the backaches so
long and they're just
sweeping it away.

DOWNHILL ALL THE WAY

I was two-and-a-half but I'd swear
I remember Leonard, the one-size-fits-all
cop next door and rides on the "rollercoaster"
(*OK if we take her? They get such a kick*)
down 11th where it dropped off TACOMA
over FAWCETT in the blue police van
with his daughters as large as loud
as he was and guys from the force all for one
free for all down to MARKET to MARKET to BUY a FAT
HOG we hollered (*a very verbal child* the doctor
told my mother and father, *keep her busy*)
so they let me go   off BROADWAY
peaking early we lurched and soared
the cops and daughters   hearts
under arrest   one crest to another   the g-force
for law and order   the law of momentum
order of streets   LookOUT
HERE COMES COMMERCE he'd bellow
while I swore up and down Watchit mister
or yulcatch a NASSfull of Radiator
and he laughed Leonard roared driving
just the right speed   JEEZus keyRYST
whynchou LOOK whereyer Going   WhattheHELLryou Doing
you CRazyBAStard
                        all songs daddy taught me
when he didn't know I could sing
the words waited anyway   bridges and backstops
or rocks (they meant nothing but *action*
some changed the world's motion, the shape
of my mother's mouth, my father's eyes)
Tacoma to Fawcett to Market to Broadway
to Commerce all the way to the flat

PACIFIC: the staid Union Station, green dome
and grey water beyond.

Last time I saw Leonard my grandpa
was dead and I'd given up
swearing   I blushed
when he asked did I still
not at fifteen

But I've taken it up   ONE MORE TIME
BUDDY and I'll RAM that DeeSOto
off the crest, launching UPYOUR (all cars
were DeSotos then, so much simpler)
Every now and again I still feel like hitting
the high points at just the right speed
I want something flying and fast
all laughing   the world falling out
from under the stomach the fear left
behind   gathering dusk and nowhere
to go but down in the lavender light
to the water with just enough breath
knowing all the right words.

BALANCING ACTS

WOODWORKING

My student says he cannot write.
There's nothing to say.
He sounds dumb on paper,
can't work with the flat white
page—not like wood, he says—
makes all his own furniture,
every room different.

All solid. He hates veneer.
The wood knows where it belongs
he mumbles. He can tell.
I want to know *how*—by grain,
by texture? There is oak in the kitchen,
walnut in the living room—
he can't explain. His smile
is deep, waiting. I look
for a pattern: *oak for sustenance,*
walnut for sharing.
He says the bedroom is purpleheart,
the hardest wood known.
Carvers don't like it.
Chisels and gouges fall apart.
Saws are ruined. But the color
is red, is rich, and he could use
the school's saw, could save his own.

Look, I say, you've made a surface.
Now give me a shape, a purpose, the sound
of the saw, the pulse in your gut
singing *risk* and *good*, your fear
for the money, the saw, for the heart
of the wood. Open the names.
Give me the terms of the trade.
You've done the hard part, the planning

and shaping. The rest is polish.
I'll help you. It's easy.
Remember to take these—
they're *your* words, I say.

But when he's gone,
the words in the wood
stand before me: *purple* for royalty,
for sweet fruit and bruises,
for blood. For bombast.
In the *heart*: passion,
intuition, love, loyalty.
And taken together: action, valor.
Decoration. I must cut through
this block, not knowing
what use, what reason, what lies
ahead to be stained and varnished.
And I set to work
saying nothing.

TRAVELING INCOGNITO

On holidays here you are again, sleeping
in stations, saver of tickets and tags
to put with your face, waiting
for your name to be called.
Here you go, shuffling credit cards
and fanning ID, smiling at perfect
strangers. You are often mistaken
for someone they know.

Weekdays you define *persona*.
Your students find you difficult
to follow, find you trying on their faces
behind their backs. You riddle your mother
constantly: I have three mouths, one
for speaking two for feeling three for giving
birth. Who am I? You are running
in circles and where do you begin you don't know
where you stand which direction to leap
to the next larger ring. You catch yourself
chanting aloud when you think you're alone:
find it find it find it. You deprive your lover
of sleep, make your body a test, exhibit
your symmetry, the lights and shadows,
an ink blot: What do you see? what do you make
of me? You have always been a mistress
of disguise.

Lately you are afraid you have gone too far,
even your dog has lost track and friends want to help you
out of your present getup into something more
comfortable, into one more becoming.
Not even mirrors give you away. You cling
to the cries of saleswomen: It's YOU!
Oh yes, it's *you*, under all this pink

netting, these feathers, under the rice and white
lace, the camisole and black garters, calling yourself
to order. You in the fishnet
stockings the velveteen drapes, beneath the mortar-
boards and orchids, the Indian cotton faded
overalls the cords and polo shirts the blues,
the greens, the bubblegum and sequins, packing
and unpacking, knowing you must
get down to where you started,
to where you meet yourself,
coming back.

DIVINING

That winter you misplaced yourself, no one
knows why your flesh came off the way
it did, pleating towards your ankles
like a collapsing concertina, or why
your face went slack before the rest.

When they found you, tightly furled
inside the concrete pipe, your ears
were lined with teeth, your lips
had been thrown a short distance
away, one eye was set in the cup
at the base of your throat. Only
your hands were still in place, veins
tangled, the nailbeds dry, palms down,
pointing the way you had come.

No one knows how hard you shrugged
to fit in, stammering charms to keep your head
from rolling where your arms couldn't
reach, how hard you tried to keep
everything in one place—only to be
shaken out of your cylinder like some child's game
and divined
and reassembled.

ELEGY FOR TWO YOUNG ROBINS

I.

At first all I knew was hunger, their hunger
and the parent birds taking turns, one returning
with a beetle or loops of worm in its yellow beak
poking it down into darkness
into clamor and finally quiet

until the next feeding. Then the two
open mouths two ruddy diamonds edged in bright
yellow the signal for food   more
food the parents thin and ragged always watchful
careful to stop at the wall, the wire, the cedar before

the two wavering heads pinched throats the blind heads
insisting on light on air on a world of beetles and worms
and good warm dark
                        then one stopped fighting
one head was lower, was fed less often
and *chil, il, il, il, il* was the call outside the nest
one slaty head thrust up to be fed and warmed
and kept secret. Until that daybreak

when the robins' carol turned to scolding
to warning to a call I had never heard   a battle cry
keen in the gritty dawn   an answer
to crow or cat or wind   to all the shapes of darkness
that rob nests: *we go on.*

II.

I have never liked robins:
drab and stolid, their wit accidental,
even the touted red breast is rusty,

more orange, and what sounds in the name!—
the sulking vowels the plodding
syllables *raw* and *been*   where is the music the lift
about them   how often I've cursed their loud long
braided song at daybreak, their unwelcome challenge
to *cheerily cheerup* in earliest spring before I'm ready
to listen
                but I couldn't help watching
the mating pair so close to the glass
in our front window, bringing moss and stems and litter
and mud to one shoulder of the stooped pyracantha
the firethorn   building with beaks a ragged hat
smoothing and lining the crown
                                    we couldn't help
wondering whether the tree would hold steady
whether the wires anchored to the house, the cables that whined
and whickered in any wind like nightmares would keep
the birds secure and we could give no warning
not the nervous *cuk cuk* the robins gave
from another tree when anyone neared the nest
                                    but it was calm
when they built, longer morning when she laid her eggs
and all of us looked forward
to the first brood.

III.

May Day and my husband finds half
of a robin's egg on the deck, the end
pierced, the shell and membrane pressed
inward, holding nothing. May again
my birth month and a robin flies to death
under the red van ahead of me   there is nothing
I can do   no one's fault   *robins fly low*   it is their nature
he says and despite our cars our cats we are lesser
evils   they thrive around us, choose to share
our shelter   they are common   raise two broods

each spring   they survive   it is still
early   there is time   I know

but we watched two live, begin
to grow and in dreams they return: twice the mother
has come back to show me through the glass
to let me know her children
are still possible   my husband asks
have I seen the young robins in the yard
as big as the parents now but their breasts
are buff and spotted, they are learning
to cock heads to look for worms to bathe—
have I seen them?—they are comical he says
to watch *there are other windows   it was a bad place*
to nest   he says *they should never have built*
there and he touches me   but the muted words
the sorry words break off   come to nothing
the rotting nest means *this happens sooner*
or later   means *this is always*
the danger.

Early fall, the pyracantha is heavy
with berries, ripe orange-red berries and robins
feasting on the fruit   keeping their balance
stripping the branches while the nest
falls to nothing the tree swaying
with the weight of robins and the season
is past   what grows now
is outside of us, is removed
what must be borne
is emptiness.

THE COMING OF AGE

Who could take her in?
She was eighty-seven and lived
alone (a son in ground long left
behind, two husbands gone,
three daughters grown).   What if
she fell, what if she burned,
what if she called and no one
heard? Quick or cold—
no one would know,
who could be sure if she laughed
or cried. What if she napped
and sipped and watched.
What if she died.

We closed the house: we mowed
the lawn, we drew the curtains
one last time and shut the light out
from the room where succulents
and violets grew that drop and die.
The tom comes keening
for his food. All small dangers
gone for good.

Here the lost are found
finally lost. There is a woman
who sang and swore, who gave
and gathered, who held the center.
Here lie the bodies
of other dreams: the one who begs who
cries who screams.
Here the white drifts
from bed to bed, the colors fade
in flesh and blood.

Great-Grandma was eighty-nine.
A tumor stilled her tongue.
Her will was gone,
Her caring done,
And strangers came too often.

Give us at last a gentle life,
And give us our deaths
As we forgive our daughters

For keeping us too late, too long.
Let them deliver us
Home.

FOR GRAM, APRIL 6

I promised myself
I wouldn't be
                you
wouldn't turn
                into you
wouldn't keen
and keep track
of the birth
                days
the death days
and now here it is
five years
and your number
still in my book

it's not the dying
that's hard
                enough
but the long missing
the longing the still being
dead
        all these years
that hurts that haunts me
no fair my daughter
would say
                if only
you could visit now
and then on holiday
or call
        occasionally
but then you

already do.

Kay wanted to get the best ride of anyone.
    —The Snow Queen

I.

It begins with a Handsome
(and clever) as always showing off
for his buddies until Happily Ever.
It begins with a Queen (a governing body)
and a chance to fly behind her sleigh.
And along the way there's his childhood sweetheart
bright as a pansy (but such innocence
is hard to come by).

Since the devil dropped his looking-glass
our hero Kay has been less
than Charming. Two splinters struck:
one hardened his heart   one darkened
his vision   he couldn't help it
at least that's his version.
There are three sides in all:
It's Once Upon a girl or a woman
for a boy with a bit of the devil in him.
It always starts with a Beautiful
Bad One a Beautiful Good One and a boy
who wants the best ride of anyone.

Good little Gerda's a vague sort
of beauty—very supportive though slightly
binding—but her badness Her Majesty
is tall cool and creamy, at ease in white
satin, blond but not brassy.
                    Kay couldn't wait
to follow her lead (Gerda will claim

he couldn't see straight because of the splinters)
but he saw her all right:
the fast sleigh the furs and that smile
said *how brave* and *hold on* and *more
than you know* meaning *never enough*
and the chill felt fine and her laugh
promised all.

Leaving Gerda out in the cold alone.
So Gerda the pure the loyal the lost goes
to the ends of the earth without shoes
asking the river *have you seen*
and the lonely old woman with magical
powers and talking flowers *is he well?*
She asks the crows *where* and *how
long ago* which leads to the prince
who might have been and his kind princess
and a robber's daughter who lets her go
free and a Laplander and a Finnish Lady
and everyone helps her everyone blesses
her love her weakness.
                          It's never a question
of who deserves him but which one gets him
in the Ever and Ever.
                          Gerda finds him at last
at the Snow Queen's place where he's having his ice
cream and eating it too and she starts to cry:
her tears melt his heart and wash out
the splinter. She starts to sing
and his tears clear his sight.
So Kay beats the devil and goes on to marry
and own the world and the rest
is his story.

II. *Gerda*

One minute I swear he's with me
in our own little garden high above
the street and the next thing I know
he has something in his eye
he has heartburn he says I whine
I'm stupid I'm such a baby
(he's always teasing he's not
himself) but he won't play fair
won't play with me. Then I hear
                              he's off
with the big boys and off with *her*
leaving me high and dry, not sure
if he's living or dead or which is best
and what can I do but pose here empty-eyed
in pastels and wait. It's no fun
playing helpless for crones and crows
and Laplanders and ladies if I end up
barefoot and *alone*.
                    Where's the credit
what's the point if I don't get the white
dress the roses and the big cake
when all this is over why should *she* get to wear
all the best clothes and she's been around—
she'll play him for the biggest flake
of all before she's done and remember
she's so much older.
                    But what about me?
He used to think childlike was charming
and anyway I'm good-looking I'm filling out
you think it's easy winning miss
congeniality, offending no one sometimes
all I wanted was a warm
bath was to go home and give him
up for lost for good but I've put years
into this, ages it seems

between these outsized covers
                              saving myself
when no one else would and don't forget
everyone's on my side: our friends our parents
even our grandmothers (I couldn't do it
alone) and all the mothers in the village agree
it's time he settled down, enough
of this running around, so she has a nice
figure probably nothing upstairs
and what makes him think she won't get bored
won't throw him back she doesn't need
a playmate.
                Sure she gives him crystals
and equations but can she prune roses can she bake
a cherry pie can she sew for him or know him
as long as well in sickness and in health no matter
how hard how cold how nasty he is the way
I do   I do   I do

III.   *The Snow Queen*

These days you're damned
if you do (he'll say he's blue
he has this cold, his heart's
not in it) and damned if you don't
(you're unfeeling, you're made
of ice, you're not normal)
                              after you taught him everything
he knows   who asked him to hitch that ride   to fall
asleep in your arms   who needs it and who stayed home nights
waiting for him to grow up   who watched him flex
his gift for logic   he's an expert at picking
your brain   using your body your heart
against you   who needs him
                              you promised yourself
never again the last time and here you are
just because he can spell can make words dance

he thinks you owe him the world
and a pair of skates   just listen
he acts like you keep him by force
like it was all your idea and he went along
for the ride   at the start he said *most perfect*
and *brilliant*   when you kissed him it was *crystal-
clear*   he liked a woman with spirit   *exquisite*
when you wrapped him in bearskin
he thought he'd die   then he wasn't afraid
of anything
                    but now it was just a snow
job   when you hold him he feels snowed under snowed in
you've heard it before from these young men
these boys with dark lashes and hard cheeks   next
he'll tell you there's someone else   she needs him
she looks up to him makes him feel
                                    like a king and he wants
his freedom   as though you had it to give
his latest word is *love*   he plays with it
let him find it and keep it if he can   who does
he think he is does he think
                    he's doing you a favor
teaching you a lesson
                    you'll learn someday
his last word is *frigid* and he ought to know   he is
the handsome prince   he is coming
to wake you up   to tell you
your name.

MADWOMAN IN THE BASEMENT

I.

It's a popular story: the woman of the house
a rumor, the rumor all eyes and white
nightdress, all eyes like the night
predators or the nightmares
chasing their white breath through the dim
kingdoms *by sleep by screams the pounding*
the beautiful nightshade beside herself
in moonlight, wailing curses *by dust by dead*
rats against the day against
all her days the unending house-
work, the unkind nurse, uneasy
servants—so hard to get
help, to get good women
especially   if it's not the maid
it's the governess she'd have to watch
him she'd have to fire
them all first the bed-
clothes then the bride-
clothes   she'd have to take
the veil *yes he* would *do that wouldn't he   try*
to replace her   make her live
elsewhere but she'd show him *by light by heat*
torching the damask, gutting the household
to have and to hold
for all time.

II.

At first she was subtle: a tap, a rattle
at the shutters, chatter from the sash, room for doubt
at the edge of the glass.
                    Tonight she is more

herself: stairs whine the doors report

                                        she's come down

to this deep this dampness   the last dark
unwinding   the mangle her mother her father
the vise

                so he thinks she's beneath him

the floorboards mutter   she will live in this basement
forever does he hear

                         the beams screech forever

if she wants to   it's her house her husband
he is still her husband   her lover her father
where are they   her mother her brothers
who could resist her   a beautiful jewel do you hear
no one could help it   the years the scars
she'll show him   so much taken from her
the walls give her up

                      they all let her down

to this dull air brown light
the heat vents crying   what's left   she must live
with the long-empty cages the baskets hats drapes musty
linens all things the dead left her

                           she'll learn

to live where the cartons stand for *hold*
the crates *protect*   where her hundreds of shoes
point the way   the first step toward staying
at last going nowhere

                          yes she'll treat him his new love

to flapping and clawing to dead rats to nothing
but dust to dust   the stairwell answers *my own*
my own   he has to remember   she gave him the best
years   never forget   and she's dying
how can he love someone else
this young one   *bed her quickly*   the latch snaps
old man old man   I want

                      what is mine

this house this man all fuel
for her thought her curse *taking back I take*

back this love this life this cold
night she'll go out in a blaze take them
with her   from the hearth the grate
screams *I want what is*
mine   what is
mine

III.

My part in this is simple:
I came to work and came to love—
because he had wit and warmth and his need
was plain, was like my own.
The sure line of his jaw, the pulse
at his throat said *love,*
I have love to give and his wife left him
alone.
        Then I learned his wife
didn't want him, didn't want anyone else
to have him, *learned what you don't know*
can burn you but I can't seem to stay
away,
        I keep hearing his voice   my name
on the wind and I come back in time
for the final chapter
the start of our lives
together
            only this time
when I find him in his chair, helpless
with understanding, half blind and single-handed
against the dusk, she hasn't gone up
as promised. She's at home in the ruins,
in the open at last, waiting for me
to take her in.

THE LOVE SONG OF CLEVER ELSA

I.   She Is Married

They had a daughter.
"It's not enough to hear
the flies cough and see the wind
skip up the street," said her mother.
"She must be married."
"Yes," said her father.
They were worried
no one would have her
(or she'd have no one
in a kinder translation)
because she was clever.

At last a man came to dinner.
He came from a distance
to woo their daughter,
to see if she had sense
and were truly clever—
or else Hans wouldn't want her.
"Of course, you'll see," said her mother.
"We call her clever Elsa.
She gets it from me.
Did you have enough dinner?
You must be thirsty."

They sent Elsa below for beer
and while it rushed into the pitcher—
so that her eyes would not be idle,
so that her mind wouldn't dawdle—
she looked all around.
She studied the ground and every wall
and overhead, directly above her,
found a pickax the masons had left

in the rafter by accident.
Then clever Elsa understood
  death in the beam
  dark in the wood
and began to lament:

  "If Hans and I marry
  and have a baby
  and when he's bigger,
  send him to the cellar
  to draw some beer
  and the pickax above
  comes down on his head,
  it will sever our love."

Upstairs they waited awhile,
then sent the girl
to see what kept their daughter.
Elsa told her the story
of Hans and the baby
and how he was killed
and the girl sank to the steps and wailed
as loudly as Elsa or louder.

Next the boy was sent after the pair.
Elsa told him what she'd told the maid:
  the chance   the joy
  the child   the blade
and love and life all shattered.
So the beer and their tears overflowed
till her mother came down to find out the matter
and finally the father,
his throat even tighter and dryer
and no one for company but this stranger,
went after the woman, the boy
and the girl who'd followed his daughter.
When he heard, he sobbed louder

than the rest.   They all agreed
she was a clever Elsa indeed.

At long last her suitor
thought to inquire
why they were all weeping
on the stairs to the cellar
and what was keeping the beer.

                    "Oh my dear
Hans, if we marry each other
and have a child and when he's older,
we send him down to draw the beer
and the pickax the workers left up there
dashes his brains out—isn't that reason
to weep forever?"

"Come now," said Hans,
"I could not require
more understanding than this
for my household." And ever
a man of decision and action,
he took Elsa upstairs and married her.

II.   The Rest of the Story

I awaken caught
in a fine net of fear,
too far from morning,
and strain for the light.
My head is ringing.
I was a stranger I cry
I lost you   you left me
I can't remember but I
was lost   someplace familiar
but no house was mine

You gather me in,
face against shoulder,
salt tears on salt skin.
You must understand my love
I say   *you were gone*
I was alone
look at the time
how long do we have
and how will I live
when your time comes
swinging its blade
to cut short our joy

There's a story, you say—
Grimm, you think—of a woman
whose worry killed content.
Something in a rafter—
a hatchet? a hammer? you don't
recall, but she feared
it would fall and strike
her lover. And all the time
all she had to do was take
down the hatchet or whatever.
Your smile brings me back.

                    Some time later
            Elsa went out
            to cut the corn to make the bread
            because her husband said she should
            while he went out to work for money.
            She took some stew to make the day
            go faster and warmer and as she stood
            in the fecund field, Elsa asked herself
                    Now what shall I do?
                    Shall I reap first or eat first?
            Her answer was *eat.*
            So she ate the stew

and when she was full, wondered
once more, *Now what shall I do?*
  Shall I reap first or sleep first?
  All right, I will sleep first.
So Elsa lay down
and the day was gone.

Hans waited at home.
When his wife did not come
at suppertime, he thought,
What a clever Elsa I have
who works so hard
she forgets to eat.
When the light guttered
he went to the field
but found Elsa asleep
and the corn uncut.
Then it was late,
too late to reap,
so he brought a bird-net
covered with bells
and threw it on Elsa
and went home to wait.

Finally she woke
at the bottom of dark
and stood and shook
till all the bells jangled.
Then each step she took
brought her closer to doubt:
Am I clever Elsa or not?
she cried to the night.
I'll go home she thought
Hans is sure to know.
But the door was locked.
She shouted at the window
Is Elsa within?

The rest is well known:
He answered *yes*
so Elsa was lost
and all doors closed against
her fear and his answer.
She ran away and since then
no one has seen her.

Remember, you say,
remember our love.
I carry your life
as well as my own.
How could I lose you
or lose myself?
You are not Hans.
There is no cellar
in this good house.
The child we might have made
is already dead.
It is the wrong story.
There is no need
to worry.

Yet my husband my home
I remember the ending.
You married me
for my understanding.
For now we cross years
with a touch,
a whisper, my reach
is enough to quiet
the ringing night
and still that woman
cries at the light
who will know me
when you are gone
and how can I recall

each fold and rise, the salt
and sweet of spirit and body
how keep whole
that rich unwritten glossary
for my love my love
the ax must fall.

REVENGE

TRUTH AND BEAUTY

My husband's exwife calls my mother to say she is
beautiful   she has always been
beautiful but it's so much harder
now she's dying   she says
I wish her dead   I'm mean   but my mother says not
true   I couldn't wish anyone dead and it's
true   I couldn't
                    but my husband's exwife
says we knew all along she was dying   she's forgotten
screaming how her lover found her
irresistible   she was so beautiful   how my   he was her
husband then   didn't even try to win her back and now
she's dying she's been dying for years for love
of beauty and is dying now for my husband
to call her   he promised she says in sickness
and in health until death
                            but she goes on
dying she does it beautifully   more truly
than ever before.

SERIOUS SUICIDE

Not the wan tight-lipped wound
                        the line drawing
at the wrist that begs forgiveness, not the stockpiled
pills and penitent phonecalls
                        the held the withheld
breath the drunken or drowsy afterthought
                                    but just once
if you only knew—
                you only living to die
another day—you are dying
to die
        if only you knew how

you must be more expansive, more open to beauty
and mystery
                not reproach not punishment but the ultimate self-
indulgence, self-expression
                        open yourself
to what lies below the surface of your thought your wish

come true: the slack sickle of the boning knife
making its point, unhurried, with no sheath
of philosophy beyond what can be discovered now,
at this beginning, casting off
from the *sternum*, starting beneath the heart
of the matter and drawing down, shallowly at first,
past *epidermis* the false skin into *derma*
                                or *true skin*
closer to truth, to finding yourself than you have ever been
before, forming the stem of the last incisive Y more carefully
than any pathologist, the good salt blood following
your progress
                down, past all gut feeling, drawing
deeper, closer still to the visceral you,

now branching out, folding back the flap, reaching
layer by layer:
                    the *fascia* superficial and deep,
the shining sheath of muscle, and coyly now,
lifting the *omentum majus*, the lacy apron
to reveal the lap of luxury, the seat of all
your learning, the shimmering coils in their basin
of bone—once out, the gift
that won't fit its box, that will never go back
the same way, there will have to be new
arrangements—
                    and there you are
delivered, cradling yourself in your lap, sole possessor
of a new certainty:
                    the rest of your life.

After her tousled
   and faintly blowsy mis-
spent youth (spent on penny
   candy red meat and roadkill
coats on that improbable
   hair the color
of raw sugar)
              after a brief darker
stint with Messrs. Not Too
   Bright Not Too Big and Too
Cold (see *Goldilocks and the Three*
   Bores) followed
by a disastrous heldover engagement
   (See *Goldilocks and the*
Three Beers) to Mr. Not Too Hot
   she settled
             down with Mr. Just
Right whose charming kiss off
   center was not too wet not
too dry but not just now
            Barely
roused she found herself
   trading 4 on the floor for 3
on the tree (see
   Goldilocks and the Three Gears)
trading one bedroom first last
   and deposit (see *Goldi-*
Locks and the Three Years) for a charming
   two story
            in a level sub-
urban planned community
   a land of beauty
bark attuned to duvet and bidet and
   covenants They (she

and J.R.) found exactly two
    model children
a mystery gift
    from some spirit at the house-
warming it all seemed so long
    long ago a land of manicured
hands and lawns
                    of rootless
longings and quiet
    punctured punctuated and pierced
only occasionally
    by stertorous snores
    by mowing and weeping
    and sewing
                bent
on achieving a Golden
                    Mean
no longer bold and brassy but
    older refined mulched
and weeded assured in certain knowledge
    of the coming
bear market.

SECOND STORY WOMAN

Pinched gable left open, the short fall
to the bed beneath. The second story is always
dark. Her knees ache in answer
to the many climbs, the angles.
She knows the owner
is home, knows he will hold out keys
misplaced when she thought she had nothing
to lose. He asks now if she's come
for more. He says admit me
to your dreams. He says it's good
to talk.

The bed is her only frame
of reference. She feels for the words: *hold*
and *know*—she must take them
back. Aloud she says all the pretty words,
want and *last*, the pretty words
have two faces. He's made them harder
to find.
He says he's tired
of her searching, says the words
were never hers, they belonged
in the first story.

Year after year she returns
to search beneath the heat, the bed,
beneath the grey walls leaning close
above her. She warns someday she'll find
the words, she won't be caught. She'll leave
the second story empty. He says all her stories
end that way.

DREAMING, AFTER ALL

For months he walked the walls wearing
your clothes: this saucer-man,
                night-blotter,
promising free fall, holding me
to my words.

I grew to find him
faintly picaresque, vaguely
familiar: all legs
and arms—snake-man,
                nettle-man,
sporting the soft belly
of nightmare, the butt
of all his own jokes.

There was no getting
around him. Finally
I opened my face to him, drew
thin boundaries where we touched,
made claims for us
alone. I gave him dim light, down
comforters and all the time

in the world. And then
he wasn't you.

LEARNING TO SHARE

You have made it my dream
too: locks that won't lock and lights
that won't light, switchplates
gone, switches gone slack
giving up
night. Room after breathless
room, I must know who it is
I can't see or keep/ out—no stranger
to the heart beating/ time,
no stranger/ to you.
                          At first
there is Grandma and food,
the food thick and dark, a friend
is pregnant. I point out death, its scent
on my skin. Great grandma leaves,
then the friend, then the cry tangled deep
in the throat. I don't know the man
holding me/ perhaps you
are not with me/ we struggle
over the story of my life: who rises
who falls/ breaks free/ who lies
who cannot scream/ over and over
the smell of death/ the darkness bears
down and you watch, knowing
how it ends, knowing all
along. The hard part
is finding myself, alone, and morning
still so far, so far.

SAME DREAM, THREE ENDINGS

The first time I descend
the staircase with the music   I say
to the camera or to anyone who'll listen   I'll
get him back   I'll think about it later
at Tara. The lighting is all
from my eyes   the eyes have it
Later   in the dressing room
I chant my mantra to the mirror
I must get him back   I will get
him back   get him back   I will
I will   I will

The second time the music goes down
without me   I know it will be
you at the door   appearing in black
& white   and I say (lighting
a long cigarette) what makes you think
I'd take you back
the words white
and dry as smoke   I'm sorry
you say and I begin
to soften   the smoke goes out
of my voice   I say   no
it wasn't you it was
the time   our eyes are full
as you turn   fade   I begin to see
through you   or rather I am seen
through you   the music starts slowly
up the stairs

The third time's the charm   there is no
music   no staircase   only this shallow stretch of night
we've been over it before   the light
yellow as an old bruise   and you

are saying I love you I'll always
love you   saying goodbye I'll always love you
and you die you
die in my arms but
you die.

REVENGE

He is calling now as you dreamed he would,
crooning *sorry* and *love* and *sorry* as you dreamed
he would when he was root and stem,
when you turned to him, held
fast at the center, all the warm
smooth length of him learning with you
your shallows your depths
and what would you have said then—
ten years before—with the ache
so sharp in your throat
but *believe* and *give*, when you wanted
your anger cut close and low, promising darkness
like the dress he hated.
You had to outdo him,
outdance him, so you have
and he's saying you're the only woman
he ever loved, he feels bad
he treated you so bad he was too young
he guesses but he hasn't been happy
since. He is still the wounded
football hero, your first kiss,
the first cock crowing
you awake. What can you say in return
but *sorry*—he sounds the same—
and *it doesn't matter anymore*
because it doesn't.

She wants your husband—
hang on—to forgive her forgive
her lover forgive the slow growth
inside her—*I'll get him*. She's calling him
to her bedside, to her hospital room
for what must be the final curtain
he must always be there always

she was his wife after all
he's a bastard he's dear
after all the raw light and faithless
dark   all the lifeless years
she wants to be his friend
will always be the love he thought
would save him and let us forgive ourselves
as we forgive those who would take love
from us—*hang on, I'll get him*—she calls
and calls and there is no answer.
Only that lost boy reaching
the wrong number.
Only that husk-woman dying again
on a different street
and the past waiting to take us
in its arms.

AIR SIGNS

SONG FOR SLOW FLIGHT

Flying is like walking
a wire   it takes
certain skill   a belief
in *here* and *there*
in going somewhere
                          no place
in particular   but the end
of a line.

It's close work   this threading
the wind   these stitches in time:
a balancing act
with counterfeit wings
cumbrous and necessary
as the steadying poles
the wiredancers carry
a kind of defiance.

The fixed wings reach
beyond what you feel
in the belly
                of space
in the lap of now
or never
            The wire is all
between you and the air
you remember in dreams
how light you were
how you floated free
and what freakish grace
what clownish beauty

you've traded fate for a moment
more above the ground
in the deep full light
for a dream of flying
where if you fall
you fall.

DREAMING DOWNWARD

We are the first generation to see the clouds from both sides.
What a privilege! First people dreamed upward. Now they dream
both upward and downward. This is bound to change something,
somewhere.
　　　　　—Henderson the Rain King

If you fly into a cloud
you must rise above metaphor,
past arbitrary signs and sins
and headings, past *sense*
and *tense* to only *senses*.
Clouds have no grammar.
Their meanings are clear:
　　　　　　　　　　　those castles
dank as wells, those stifling
scarves, the whales
spouting fire, the churning flukes,
the swell and slap of weather.

There is no softness here,
no cushion, no cotton
or raw wool, no nurture.
Only dugs that let down
but cannot sustain.
　　　　　　　If you can't get over
or under, try changing
direction: believe in the compass,
go out the way you came in.
It may be there is safer air
behind you, you may be borne again,
uplifted beyond reason.
　　　　　　　　To fly is to gain
perspective: not *my house*
but *houses*, not *some-*

where but *every*.
The narrow view of infinity.
                              In the absence
of color and volition
you must assume a horizon,
imagine one somewhere beyond
your perfect vision.
And keep *blue* in mind
(not the painted half-dome
in the attitude indicator
with its false planes,
its measured ups and downs,
those convenient lies, all grounded
in fact.) Now your eyes
that turn from green to grey
that give him pleasure
                              are useless
except to scan
the flight instruments
around and around the shrinking circumference
from gauge to gauge to meaningless
gauge, the sum of experience,
the cardinal questions:
how fast, what attitude, how high
or low and *gaining or losing,*
which way, what angle
of bank, how far from the ideal
of straight and level?

To lose track of one
answer is to let go all
pretense. There's no time
to be lonely, no up no down
only sound and tilting
the roar the whine
of the engine pulling
one wing one way

or another   no mind only body
and the sense of falling hoping
to recover your life
suspended in suspended water.

In that white instant you'll see
your future: a spiral return
to fluid, to darkness.
You will learn *gravity*.

FORCED LANDING

Take a friend along when you learn
to mount the wind. Climb until your heart forgets
the background beat of the engine.
To fly is to foil expectation, to deny rejection
above ground. Never admit
machinery. Do not even breathe
automatically. Anything taken for granted
will be taken away.
You depend on the violence of air and vapor,
on skill and Bernoulli to lift you
out of the ordinary. No matter how warm
and clear you find the day, listen
for chill: the rough sound
means ice, means loss
of power.

    Here's a chance to determine
    your fate (your birth
    just happened in painful
    silence). The glide path
    will tell you when
    to crash, to turn off
    everything and open
    your door. (That way
    when the dusty wings fold up,
    you won't be trapped.)

    You have just enough time
    for a prayer: "Let me lose
    my body, let me rob the gravesite,
    the slick grey men selling
    boxes and markers, plots
    for eternity." If your eyes
    still see, if you feel

fortunate, then walk away
from the lifeless bird,
the shattered breast,
wings more stiff than metal,

and report the accident.
Say you're sorry for any trouble.
Tell someone in charge the sky
wouldn't hold you,
the hills stopped exhaling,
fields called you down.
Learn to be gracious
accepting compliments.
Nod and say the earth
is with us always,
you have returned to rest
uneasy on its surface and your friend
helped you understand you must go alone
below ground.

ELEGY FOR A FLIGHT INSTRUCTOR

for Fil

UKIAH, Ore.—A woman part-time flying instructor from Burien, in her first air show, was killed yesterday afternoon when her plane crashed half a mile from a crowd watching her aerobatic performance. The victim was identified as Filomena Reda, 30. . . .
—Seattle Post-Intelligencer, July 3, 1977

It isn't that you went,
it's that you went without telling anyone
how long you might be gone, without filing a flight plan.
We were supposed to go up. My lesson was scheduled
in advance. For days when the phone didn't ring
I thought it was you. In dreams I struggled
with crosswinds, strained to hear your voice,
to reach narrow grass strips.
You should have canceled.

The words in the paper were clean, bloodless: "The plane
went into a spin and crashed." There was only a hint of your
descent: the sleek Decathlon turning so fast so slow closing
with its axis wing after wing furling to a leaf
to a shroud the narcotic momentum the force
pulling your face to a mask, taut-lipped, defiant—
the final dark explosion of dust.

I've pulled out of dreams before impact, gone over and over
the tricks you taught me: how to balance wind
on my wings, shoulder aside gusts, cast shadows on clouds,
black crosses on hilltops. Still,
I keep returning to rectangles, to the arrogant
patterns we traced together, falling only to learn
recovery, knowing the earth would wait.

These days the sky will not admit me.
There are more portents than I have time
to read: fine rain from an empty sky, an amber moon,
my own ragged shadow. My nails are breaking
down to the quick. "Don't be so hard on yourself,"
you said. "If *I* can do it, so can you."
You showed me how to maintain altitude, how to fight
to stay on course, making small corrections constantly.

Why didn't you warn me, you who could read the signs—
thickening air, rising darkness, the shattering ripeness
of trees—that fall would come early
this year? What were you thinking? giving up time,
dimension, giving yourself to the eddy, knowing the horizon
lost, knowing some would hold you up
as an example, a blot on your perfect record,
knowing I wasn't ready to fly alone, knowing
what I didn't know.

HOLDING PATTERN

At first it's hold short
of the runway, taxi into position
and hold. Then it's touch
and go all the way,
trees nodding below, the sky
open to you, the soft splintered
light, everything in its old place, the land-
marks showing the side you grew up with, the same
shades of hills, at a safe distance the anvil
clouds, the fitting chorus of thunder, in the plush
folds beneath your tongue an ode to every
direction of wind, to the dense rush
of silence.

You were not meant to stay here, close
to jet-wakes fanning like bones
in the back of your hand, things shrinking
away from your touch. The man in the tower
calls you down. You are no longer
in control. Entering to the south the pattern
is always the same: left turn left
turn, a box of horizons, not enough sky left
to hold you, the next to the last turn
is yours, just enough fuel to reach
the nearest ground, left to final
approach. Somehow landing is always the shock
you expected.

LOVE IS IN THE AIR

When we're married, you won't expect me
to go flying *with you, will you?*
—DW

Come up and catch my aviatrix
with ailerons and rudders.
Here's lift and thrust to startle the dust
and never mind the shudders.

It's here come the cumulus
and there go the ground rules.
Then Waddayaknow and Roger Willco,
hand in hand in handfuls,

sing hi ho the thunderhead,
how high the anvil!
But steer clear of the lightning there
for a rousing ride in April.

There's What Now the passenger
and Who Knows the pilot,
arm in arm in the pelting storm,
agreeing to be quiet.

So push/pull the elevator,
don't lose the latitude.
We'll burble a while in a power-on stall
till we find the proper attitude.

Come slow flight and steep turns,
come obstacles and aircraft.
Overwego and Tally Ho,
cheek to cheek on an updraft,

roll to the left and roll to the right
and ring around a pylon:
it's tumble and pitch with the mixture rich
in jumpsuits all of nylon.

Sing how low the final approach
and oh no the windsock.
Come hey diddle diddle high over Seattle
and who's afraid of the bedrock?

It's all for the landing strip
and two for elevation,
then one last flare in the cockpit, dear,
for private aviation.

MATING RITUALS

The Song

Wherever we live   my house
finch   my linnet   in town
or city   in the open
country   wouldn't you warble
and che-urr for me?
Wouldn't you raise your crest
your bright voice   while I build
our nest of stems and paper?

We are paired for life my musical
genius   my blushing suitor
I'll give back a few notes
from your sweet variations:

Follow my love in the longing light
as the ruddy finch dances
and sings for his mate and sings
for his mate.

The Garden

Would you build me a garden my bower
bird   wouldn't you scavenge deep feathers
and ferns   stones from dead rivers
      wouldn't they glitter

then would you weave me a nuptial chamber
pavilion of sticks   courtyard of moss and quick silver
lichens
          would you summon flowers
ripe blossoms and berries   charcoal and bark

at the rim of the clearing
    would you dance for me there
display and display while I play hard
to get
      but wouldn't I enter
would I tempt you to take me under
your wings   letting the dark beat closer
and closer   wouldn't you know at last at the heart-red
bud of the world I was yours
forever.

SONG FOR THE PRESENT

Crash of rain and crows
dancing
on the roof.
You and the day
lightly
into the room.

These things happen only once.
Once again
we are here in time
for morning, another moment
gone long
before the telling.

When I close my eyes, you remain
beside me, half your face
submerged in sleep,
your body open to mine.
All the deep night I learned by heart
the slow curve of cheek, thigh, the long milling
of bones.

The words will come: *I love you, love*—old charms
against the dark. For now our bodies
know the way, teach us *hold* and *release*.
No words yet, but listen
to the little songs in the blood, my pulse
naming you, flesh recalling
flesh. We have reached this place
together, have made it warm.
We are keeping
time, keeping time.

JIGSAW PUZZLES

Sunday evening I tell my husband I want something
to do, something sedentary, I don't know
but not reading not thinking, I feel scattered, vaguely
dissatisfied—not sex not ice cream but something mindlessly
involving—not television—something for the hands
to take my mind off whatever
                          I don't know
and my husband goes out and brings me back
jigsaw puzzles: thousands of pieces of autumn
landscape and a weathered farm in cardboard
boxes and that's it, that's just
what I had in mind if I had anything
in mind. I choose the farm
because it's smaller and easier (the landscape
is all fallen or falling leaves), because it has a road
with a boy and a fawn-colored cow and their legs
will be easy to find. I start with the border,
rummage in the box for straight edges, build a frame
of reference at the same time turning all the pieces
face up, sorting and grouping: the obvious sky
the packed dirt road
                 as straight
as the road by my uncle's wheat farm that summer
the veils of heat above blacktop the guileless
grasses   I find the cow's muzzle the boy's blue
sweater   it must be late autumn late
in the afternoon there's a breeze
                      cool and full
of promise as the creek that bordered my aunt's
truck farm   here's the rusty farmhouse the barn's gaping door
    way
the place inside where light stops
                        my uncle Bill

kept cows once and chickens he was surprised I wanted
to take the warm eggs out from under wanted to ride
on the green combine because my mother didn't
when she was a kid but I needed to let go to be lifted up
to a new place a different view to trust   his hands
were hard and warm the dusty coveralls his hair wheat-
colored I wanted to touch to see everything as much
as possible all at once to belong to take
part and be myself
                          now I place the uncertain ones
together at one side   maybe the barn roof or shady part
of the driveway impossible to tell sometimes
till most of the pieces are in   maybe the path
beyond the border to the marbled fields the harvested
ones   I search by color by shape   for any clue
to what comes next   fooled by the similar   surprised
by sudden recognition   how often the mind gives up
what the eye held clear   I know the farm
the house and grounds will go quickly now
                                                    my husband
once owned part of a farm   he misses the natural
order   watching the hawks the mice in the grass everything
in its place and I miss it for him with him want it
for him   it all goes so much faster
toward the last and then it's not really a picture
you can keep   the process is all
that matters after all not the product the end
result.
            Still I pause to admire my work
before I break it down, to silently thank
the boy, the cow, and the photographer,
the puzzle company, the cutting machine.
I am thankful for pieces that fit
the larger picture   for even a glimpse
of how it turns out   grateful

for my husband   his love his knowing
what is needed   for this moment of holding
together when everything falls
into place.

AT THE BALLET

Thinking again
how I envy them
these young
         women
the touch
of a partner
the physical
        ease
and certainty

not that I want
to be lifted
into arabesque
or held to entrechat—
the fierce brief beats—
or even a fireman's
         carry
but to feel again
his hands firm
at my waist

ready

DREAMING WINTER

Only sing the moment and the sea
the raw cry of water
falling still
and *you* & *I* and *my*
and *our* mean
nothing
   my hand
smoothing
our sad bed
and winter rain
moon deep in the meat of it
         now
we wander
falter—
what words but *over*
cold swift life worn *down*
like stones
in the river.

IN PRAISE OF OPEN MOUTHS

Old men forget their mouths
are open. They leave them open to listen
not to speak. It's the first sign,
you say, of old age.

Source and *mouth*, I counter.
The long years between us cut deep
but narrow. We chose this course, this bed,
bring to it our confluence, rich and giving.

The mouth you say is the end
of a river.

I say *we sing, we wonder
we sometimes laugh*—
                        Your eyes
brown with green depths,
warm and full as the summer pond,
go dark.
            We kiss I offer.

You see yourself one day
across a white table, open-mouthed. I have to leave you
one day, you have to leave me, your breath going out
and out beyond me, my heart
a fist a rag my mouth a scar—
                        but think my love
how often we forget ourselves, how old we have become
even now, together here and now, one inside
the other inside each other our mouths

open

ABOUT THE AUTHOR

A Northwest writer, Robin Seyfried's poems have appeared in many journals. She was an editor of *Poetry Northwest* from 1978-1997 and is currently editing a fortieth-anniversary anthology of the magazine. She enjoys flying and is a licensed private pilot.

ACKNOWLEDGMENTS

These poems, some in slightly different form, have appeared in the following publications: "Hanging On," "Divining," "Elegy for a Flight Instructor," "Song for What Fell to the Floor," "Dancing Attendance," and "Same Dream, Three Endings" in POETRY NORTHWEST; "Holding Pattern" and "Second Story Woman" in TELESCOPE; "Mating Rituals: The Garden," "Mating Rituals: The Song," and "Love Is in the Air" in THE SEATTLE REVIEW; "Revenge" in SONORA REVIEW; "Bedtime Stories" and "Serious Suicide" in HANGING LOOSE; "Truth and Beauty" and "Jigsaw Puzzles" in THE AMERICAN SCHOLAR; and "The National Anthem," "The Wives of the Poets," "Poem with Questions Following," and "Bulk Poetry" in POETRY. "Elegy for Two Young Robins" is reprinted from PRAIRIE SCHOONER by permission of the University of Nebraska Press. Copyright 1985, University of Nebraska Press. "The National Anthem" was reprinted in ANTHOLOGY OF MAGAZINE VERSE & YEARBOOK OF AMERICAN POETRY, 1984 edition.

!